W9-BDV-090

INSECTS: SIX-LEGGED NIGHTMARES

GIANT WETAS SHOCK!

BY JANEY LEVY

Gareth Stevens
PUBLISHING

Please visit our website, www.garethstevens.com. For a free color catalog of all our high-quality books, call toll free 1-800-542-2595 or fax 1-877-542-2596.

Cataloging-in-Publication Data

Names: Levy, Janey.
Title: Giant wetas shock!/ Janey Levy.
Description: New York : Gareth Stevens Publishing, 2018. | Series: Insects: six-legged nightmares | Includes index.
Identifiers: ISBN 9781538212592 (pbk.) | ISBN 9781538212615 (library bound) | ISBN 9781538212608 (6 pack)
Subjects: LCSH: Giant wetas–Juvenile literature. | Grasshoppers–Juvenile literature.
Classification: LCC QL508.A56 L49 2018 | DDC 595.7'26–dc23

First Edition

Published in 2018 by
Gareth Stevens Publishing
111 East 14th Street, Suite 349
New York, NY 10003

Copyright © 2018 Gareth Stevens Publishing

Designer: Laura Bowen
Editor: Ryan Nagelhout/Kate Mikoley

Photo credits: Cover, p. 1 (giant weta) Robin Bush/Oxford Scientific/Getty Images; cover, pp. 1-24 (background) Fantom666/Shutterstock.com; cover, pp. 1-24 (black splatter) Miloje/Shutterstock.com; pp. 4-24 (text boxes) Tueris/Shutterstock.com; p. 5 Jenny & Tony Enderby/Lonely Planet Images/Getty Images; p. 7 """Joel Sartore, National Geographic Photo Ark"""/National Geographic/Getty Images; p. 9 Mark Moffett/Minden Pictures/ Getty Images; p. 11 (main) RnDmS/Shutterstock.com; p. 11 (inset) Sue McDonald/Shutterstock.com; p. 13 Nimai/ Shutterstock.com; p. 15 Barcroft Media/Getty Images; p. 17 Giantflightlessbirds/Wikimedia Commons; p. 18 Evgeny Gorodetsky/Shutterstock.com; p. 19 Brian Enting/Science Source/Getty Images; p. 20 IgorGolovniov/ Shutterstock.com; p. 21 Dinobass/Wikimedia Commons.

Printed in China

CPSIA compliance information: Batch #CW18GS: For further information contact Gareth Stevens, New York, New York at 1-800-542-2595.

CONTENTS

Words in the glossary appear in **bold** type the first time they are used in the text.

GOD OF UGLY THINGS

It lives only on islands off the coast of New Zealand. It's huge for its kind and has a thick, heavy body. It creeps about slowly in the darkness of night on **spine**-covered legs.

To some people, this **insect** looks scary. Its names show that. Its scientific name is *Deinacrida heteracantha* (dee-ihn-AA-krih-duh heh-tuh-ruh-KAN-thuh). *Deinacrida* means "terrible grasshopper." The Maori—New Zealand's native people—call it the wetapunga (way-tuh-POONG-uh) in their language. That name means "god of ugly things."

TERRIFYING TRUTHS

Wetapungas have been around for 190 million years. They walked with dinosaurs!

The wetapunga is just one of 11 different kinds of giant wetas (WAY-tuhz).

HEAVIER THAN TWO MICE!

Like all insects, wetapungas have six legs, two **compound eyes**, two antennae, and a hard covering called an exoskeleton. They also have a body with three parts: a head, a **thorax**, and an abdomen, or stomach. But unlike many insects, they don't have wings. That's because they're too heavy to fly. The "terrible grasshoppers" can't even hop!

Wetapungas can be 4 inches (10 cm) long—not including their legs and antennae. And they can weigh up to 2.5 ounces (71 g). That's heavier than two mice. Yikes!

TERRIFYING TRUTHS

Wetapungas breathe through holes in their exoskeleton. And their ears are located on their front legs!

PARTS OF A GIANT WETA

legs

spines on legs

head

abdomen

thorax

compound eye

antennae

This shows the parts of a giant weta.

WHAT'S FOR DINNER?

What do wetapungas eat to get so huge? You might think they must be carnivores, or meat eaters, to grow so big. But you'd be surprised. They actually like to dine on fresh greens!

Like grasshoppers, wetapungas are mainly herbivores, or plant eaters. However, unlike grasshoppers, people don't consider them pests. Wetapungas eat mostly leaves from many types of New Zealand trees. They prefer to eat from plants with large leaves. They also eat fruit and, occasionally, small insects.

TERRIFYING TRUTHS

Wetapungas like to eat carrots. They can bite off pieces of carrot just like you can!

It's common for people in New Zealand to feed carrots to wetapungas.

9

AT HOME IN THE TREES

If you visited New Zealand, you likely wouldn't see a wetapunga—unless you climbed a tree. That's because wetapungas spend most of their life in trees. They usually hide among dead leaves such as those of tree ferns, certain kinds of palm trees, or cabbage trees. However, female wetapungas must come to the ground to lay their eggs.

Wetapungas are **nocturnal**. They sleep while hiding in trees during the day. At night, they come out to search for food.

TERRIFYING TRUTHS

Wetapungas sometimes share their hiding places with small rats that are about the same size. Which one is scarier?

cabbage
tree

Wetapungas may live high off the
ground. Some of the trees they live
in, such as cabbage trees, may
grow to be 66 feet (20 m) tall!

DOZENS OF COUSINS

The wetapunga is just one of over 70 species, or kinds, of wetas in New Zealand. There are 10 other giant weta species, but none are as big as the wetapunga. The smallest species is the tiny Nelson alpine weta, which weighs only 0.25 ounce (7 g)!

New Zealand also has seven kinds of tree wetas, three kinds of wetas with **tusks**, eight kinds of ground wetas, and a great many kinds of cave wetas. And scientists are still finding new species!

TERRIFYING TRUTHS

You can find wetas in all sorts of habitats, including grasslands, forests, and caves. They dig holes under stones, rotting logs, or in trees.

Tree wetas belong to the same family as wetapungas, they're just not as large. But you have a much better chance of meeting a tree weta. Tree wetas are the most familiar of all wetas because they're the ones people run into most often.

tree weta

A LONG CHILDHOOD

Wetapungas start out as eggs buried deep in the ground. They hatch, or come out of their eggs, after about 10 months. The tiny new wetapungas are called nymphs. They look like little adults, but they're only about 0.2 inch (5 mm) long.

Young wetapungas must **molt** about 11 times to reach their full adult size. That's more times than most insects molt, and it can take wetapungas up to 2 years to become adults! That's a long time in the insect world.

TERRIFYING TRUTHS

A grasshopper might molt five or six times and take a month to become an adult. That's a big difference from wetapungas!

A wetapunga molting would look much like this grasshopper molting. You can see that the molted exoskeleton, shown here on the left, still holds the shape of the grasshopper!

TIME FOR BABIES

A few months after wetapungas become adults, they're ready to **mate**. Male and female wetapungas may find each other using special scents called pheromones (FEHR-uh-mohnz). After they mate, the female must come down to the ground to lay her eggs in the soil.

Female wetapungas have a special body part on the end of their abdomen called an ovipositor (OH-vuh-pah-zuh-tuhr). It allows them to lay their eggs deep in the soil, where they stay safe until the babies come out months later.

TERRIFYING TRUTHS

Female wetapungas can lay 100 to 300 eggs during their lifetime. That's a lot of baby wetapungas!

The Mahoenui giant weta, shown here, uses her ovipositor to bury her eggs about 1 inch (2.5 cm) deep in the soil. Female wetapungas can bury their eggs twice that deep!

ovipositor

IN DANGER

Wetapungas were once common throughout New Zealand's North Island. They were also found on several nearby islands. What happened? People came, and with them came animals that hunted wetapungas and **competed** with them for food.

Rats and mice hid on the ships that brought people to New Zealand. They competed with wetapungas for food and ate young wetapungas. People also brought cats, and cats found the giant insects made tasty meals. By 1900, wetapungas only survived on Little Barrier Island.

Little Barrier Island

The kiore, or Polynesian rat, is only about the size of an adult wetapunga. But when these animals arrived in New Zealand, they put the wetapunga species in danger by eating young wetapungas.

SAVING WETAPUNGAS

Today, New Zealand's Department of **Conservation** has a **breeding** program, or plan, to save wetapungas. It's working to reestablish wetapunga populations where the insects were once plentiful, but have since vanished.

The plan includes wetapungas from Little Barrier Island and groups such as the Auckland Zoo. Workers care for the wetapungas, mate them, and raise the babies. When the young are old enough, they're set free on other islands that have no predators. So far, the plan has been a success!

giant weta on a stamp

40c NEW ZEALAND

GIANT WETA

Because of predators, wetapungas will never be able to come back to the wild of New Zealand's North Island, but other species of wetas still live there. New populations of wetapungas have been established on Tiritiri Matangi Island and Motuora Island!

GLOSSARY

breeding: mating

compete: to try to win a contest with others

compound eye: an eye made up of many separate seeing parts

conservation: the care of the natural world

habitat: the natural place where an animal or plant lives

insect: a small, often winged, animal with six legs and three body parts

mate: to come together to make babies. Also, one of two animals that come together to produce babies.

molt: to shed, or get rid of, an exoskeleton

nocturnal: active at night

spine: a long, sharp body part

thorax: the part of an insect's body that holds the heart and lungs

tusk: a long, sharp body part on an insect's head

FOR MORE INFORMATION

BOOKS

Lunis, Natalie. *Giant Weta: The World's Biggest Grasshopper*. New York, NY: Bearport Publishing, 2013.

Morris, Sandra. *Welcome to New Zealand: A Nature Journal*. Somerville, MA: Candlewick Press, 2015.

Turner, Matt. *Extraordinary Insects*. Minneapolis, MN: Hungry Tomato, 2017.

WEBSITES

New Zealand Weta
nhc.net.nz/index/insects-new-zealand/weta/weta.htm
Check out lots of great weta photos on this website, including some awesome close-ups!

Wetas
wildaboutnz.co.nz/2010/12/wetas/
Learn more about wetas on this New Zealand wildlife website.

INDEX